German Sturmartillerie at War Vol.2

Text by Frank V. De Sisto
Color plates by Laurent Lecocq

Introduction

Sturmartillerie Redefined

As the Second World War continued to rage, the need to engage in combat in an urban setting continued to grow. The initial concept behind the use of the Sturmgeschütze III envisioned an "open" form of warfare, which has some essential differences compared to combat in built-up areas. For instance, during the campaign to conquer Poland in 1939, the Germans learned that the armored vehicles currently in service demonstrated limitations when fighting took place within the Polish capital city, Warsaw.

No protracted or large-scale urban combat took place during the battles in Western Europe, Scandinavia, Greece or The Balkans. The advent of Operation Barbarossa saw the Germans optimistically predicting a quick victory, with little need for battles in Soviet cities. Later of course, the harsh reality set in as a speedy outcome to the campaign rapidly receded. Then, in late 1942, as the battle for Stalingrad dragged on, the Germans cast about for a means to provide a mobile, protected gun of a relatively large caliber, with the power to demolish large structures with a single shot and the armor to withstand close encounters with enemy anti-armor weapons. Heavier armor became more important since the use of maneuver in congested cities and towns was severely restricted; these newer assault weapons often had no choice but to meet the enemy "head-on".

These requirements resulted in the design and fielding of several vehicle types, two of which mounted conventional 15cm gun/howitzers on the Pz.Kpfw.III and Pz.Kpfw.IV chassis, respectively. The third used the chassis of the Tiger I, mounting a 38cm "projector", or heavy mortar, based on a naval weapon.

In addition to designing, producing and fielding new types of Sturmartillerie (albeit based on a combination of existing designs), a "hybrid" was fielded based on components of the Sturmgeschütz III Ausf.G assault gun and the Panzerkampfwagen IV medium tank. This was an improvised design that was quickly produced when Sturmgeschütz III Ausf.G production was severely curtailed in the autumn of 1943, due to Allied air raids on the Alkett factory. It should be mentioned that the Jagdpanzer 38 was also designed and fielded to make up for this production shortfall. This should give the reader some idea of the very high value the Germans bestowed upon this vehicle type.

Sturmgeschütz IV für 7.5cm Sturmkanone 40 (L/48) (Sd.Kfz.167)

As previously-mentioned, and as was their intent, Allied air attacks had a detrimental effect on German AFV production, including the highly-regarded Sturmgeschütz III Ausf.G. Within days of the end of a series of raids in the autumn of 1943, German designers grafted the casemate and main gun of the StuG.III Ausf.G to the chassis of the Pz.Kpfw.IV Ausf.H and later the Ausf.J. The casemate was butted-up against the engine compartment firewall and also raised above its normal position resting on the track guards. This required that the area beneath and in front of the casemate be enclosed with new plates. The driver's compartment remained in the same position as on the Pz.Kpfw.IV, so a new armored extension was grafted on to the front of the casemate. This included a pair of periscopes for the driver's vision while buttoned-up, and a hatch lid for his entry and egress.

As an improvisation, the StuG.IV certainly showed some creativity, but there were some trade-offs in performance. The most notable difference between the StuG.IV and the StuG.III Ausf.G was their respective combat-loaded weights; the StuG.III Ausf.G weighed 23.9 metric tons, and the StuG.IV 25.9 metric tons. This apparently did not affect mobility as the StuG.IV had roughly the same operational speed envelope and greater range than the StuG.III Ausf.G. The larger size of the StuG.IV allowed for better crew comfort as well as more ammunition stowage than the StuG.III Ausf.G.

The StuG.IV incorporated many, if not all, of the incremental improvements introduced to the Pz.Kpfw.IV chassis, to include the Flammvernichter (flame-dampening exhaust) pipes; three, instead of four return rollers; hull side plates extended to be used as tow-hook brackets, and the addition of a bracket to the center of the rear hull plate to mount an articulating tow hook.

The StuG.IV casemate also received the same upgrades as seen on standard StuG.III Ausf.Gs. These included the introduction of Nahverteidigungswaffe (close defense weapon) and Rundumfeuer (360-degree traverse MG mount). No photographs have surfaced showing the Sturmgeschütz IV using the slab-sided welded mantle for the StuK40 main gun; all were apparently fitted with the cast Topfblende (pot handle) mantle. Likewise, no evidence exists to show that the StuG.IV was ever fitted with a 10.5cm Sturmhaubitze.

A total of 1,141 Sturmgeschütz IVs were built from December of 1943 to April of 1945. Most were assigned to form 10-gun Kompanien in Infanterie-Divisionen. Some went to the 90.Panzergrenadier-Division in Italy, and Pz.Abt.8, an independent formation which was deployed on the Ostfront. Waffen-SS formations also received the Sturmgeschütz IV, including 4.SS-Polizei-Division, 5.SS-Panzer-Division "Wiking", both on the Ostfront, and the 17.SS-Panzergrenadier-Division "Gotz von Berlichingen" in the west; the latter fielded an entire Abteilung in lieu of Panzer.

As mentioned above, the Sturmgeschütz IV had a combat weight of 25.9 metric tons. Its overall length was 6.7-meters, height 2.2-meters and width 2.95-meters. The Maybach HL120 TRM 12-cylinder gasoline engine propelled the vehicle to a top speed of 38kmh, out to a range of 220km, on roads. Up to 87 rounds could be stowed internally for the StuK40, which was directed using the Sfl.Z.F.1a sight. The secondary armament, either a 7.92mm MG34 or MG42, had a reserve of 2,650 rounds. Up to two MP40s were stowed for crew self-defense and the standard radio fit was a Fu.15 or Fu.16.

s.IG33 auf Fgst.Pz.Kpfw.III (Sfl.)

This series of assault guns was manufactured on re-built Sturmgeschütz III chassis as a direct result of the combat raging in and around Stalingrad. Conceived on September 20, 1942, the first of 24 Sturminfanteriegeschütze was accepted on October 13, a mere 23 days after the idea was born.

The Sturminfanteriegeschütz mounted a 15cm s.IG33/1 infantry gun on a limited-traverse mount inside a box-shaped casemate. It carried 30 rounds for the main gun and also had a ball-mounted MG34 on the superstructure front plate; this was supplied with 600 rounds. Communications were based on the Fu.Spr.d radio and an intercom system for the crew. With a combat loaded weight of 21 metric tons, it was propelled by a Maybach HL120 TRM gasoline engine, which produced 265 hp at 2600rpm. Top speed on a road was 20km per hour, while range was 110km.

The casemate's frontal armor was based on 50mm plates with additional bolted Zusatzpanzer (appliqué armor) plates that were 30mm-thick. The casemate's side armor was 50mm thick; the roof 20mm thick. Two hatch lids were provided on the rear of the casemate, while another was seen on the roof. An oblong cut-out in the roof was covered by an oval plate, spaced above it by struts. This allowed the standard gunner's sight, the Sfl.Z.F.1, to cover an arc of traverse of only six degrees; elevation was -3 degrees, + 25 degrees.

The chassis was based on various vehicles that had been returned for factory overhauling; photos show these resembling types that were produced before the 8/Z.W. chassis (Pz.Kpfw.III Ausf.J) became standardized. The s.IG33 had a base armor of 50mm on the bow and glacis plates, which was a standard feature of the Sturmgeschütz (but not the Pz.Kpfw.III until the Ausf.J), so it may be deduced that they were based on re-built assault guns. 30mm Zusatzpanzer (appliqué armor) plates were bolted to the bow and glacis.

The first 12 Sturminfanteriegeschütze were issued in lots of 6 each to Sturmgeschütz-Abteilungen 177 and 244, where (by November 1942) they formed a single 4.Batterie in each unit. These fought at Stalingrad, all eventually being destroyed or captured (one survives today at the Kubinka Museum, Moscow, Russia). The second batch of 12 served as part of XVII.Armeekorps in Sturm-I.G.-Batterie Lehr Btl. XVII and were used in the attempt to relieve the 6.Armee in and around Stalingrad. By April of 1943, the 7 remaining s.IG33s were assigned to Panzer-Regiment 201 of 23.Panzer-Division, where they made up a single Stu.I.G.-Batterie.

Sturmgeschütz IV für Sturmhaubitze 43 (Sd.Kfz.166)

Based on the same idea that spawned the previously-described s.IG33 auf Fgst.Pz.Kpfw.III (Sfl.), this Sturmpanzer was a more refined design based on the Pz.Kpfw.IV chassis. It was armed with a purpose-built 15cm StuH43 in a limited-traverse ball mount, installed in a casemate with 100mm of armor on the front plate. The 15cm main armament was supplied with up to 38 rounds, while the final version also had a 7.92mm MG34 in a ball mount on the casemate's front plate; this was supplied with 600 rounds. There were four production series', numbered I to IV, with a total of 306 being produced from April 1943 to March 1945.

3

The I.Serie Sturmpanzer was based on re-built Pz.Kpfw.IV chassis, including some as early as the Ausf.E. The vehicles in this initial series were characterized by the use of a driver's visor taken from the Tiger I, mounted on an extension of the front casemate plate. This version also featured welded armored guards over the two ventilators situated at the rear corners of the casemate. Suspension components were upgraded by the addition of dished drive sprockets, welded tube idler wheels and widened road-wheels, first introduced on the Pz.Kpfw.IV Ausf.F. Schürzen (skirts) were fitted to combat the effects of Soviet infantry anti-tank rifles.

The II.Serie version featured a longer armored sleeve on the 15cm StuH43 main weapon as well as the reinforced final drive and its associated drive sprocket first introduced on the Pz.Kpfw.IV Ausf.H. The smaller cylindrical exhaust muffler introduced on the Pz.Kpfw.IV Ausf.F was also fitted to the hull rear.

The III.Serie added a new welded hood to the front of the casemate with a single rotating periscope for the driver. An exhaust fan was added to the casemate roof to evacuate powder fumes from the fighting compartment.

The IV.Serie introduced a completely re-designed casemate. This consisted of single-piece side plates, a ball-mounted MG34 installed in the casemate face above the driver's station and a commander's cupola with periscopes, of the type fitted to the StuG.III and StuG.IV, added to the roof. Some photos show a pedestal-mounted anti-aircraft MG fitted on (or next to) the cupola ring. The casemate roof also featured a new hatch lid arrangement, new sliding gun-sight cover and a second ventilator fan added over the ball-mounted MG34. An extension of the casemate was also built over the port-side of the engine deck; this incorporated a two-part hatch lid. The suspension was eventually fitted with Gummigefederten Stahllaufrollen (rubber-cushioned steel-tired road-wheels) and the later cast idler wheel. Flammvernichter (flame-dampening exhaust) pipes were also fitted to the hull rear, in lieu of the cylindrical exhaust muffler.

The Sturmpanzer IV was organized in Abteilung strength, with 14 guns per Batterie/Kompanie and three in the Abteilung-Truppe. This gave a total of 45 guns.

Of the four Abteilungen eventually formed, the first unit, Sturmpanzer-Abteilung 216, saw service as part of s.Panzerjäger-Regiment 656, alongside the Ferdinand tank destroyer at Kursk, in July 1943. After re-fitting, Stu.Pz.Abt.216 was deployed to Italy in February, 1944 to counter the Allied landings at Anzio. The Abteilung remained in Italy until the end of the war in April, 1945.

Sturmpanzer-Abteilung 217 was sent to Normandy in July, 1944, where it was partially destroyed at Falaise; the remnants of the unit went to Holland, and later fought at Aachen, Germany. Stu.Pz.Abt.217 was deployed in the Ardennes offensive as part of 6.Panzer-Armee. After the Allied counter-offensive, the Abteilung retreated into Germany where it surrendered in the Ruhr pocket in April, 1945.

Sturmpanzer-Kompanie z.b.V.1/218 first saw action in August 1944 during the suppression of the Polish Armiya Krajowa (Home Army) in the Warsaw Uprising. In January, 1945 the Kompanie was used to form Sturmpanzer-Abteilung 218; this establishment was incomplete, and at time of its surrender, '218 was part of Kampfgruppe Großdeutschland. A sister unit, Sturmpanzer-Kompanie z.b.V 2/218 was sent to Paris in August, 1944.

The final unit to be formed, Sturmpanzer-Abteilung 219, was established in September, 1944; by December of that year, it was deployed to Hungary. In January, 1945, it went to Budapest with the 23.Panzer-Division. By March, it was re-equipped and sent to Czechoslovakia, where it surrendered at war's end.

The Sturmpanzer IV was powered by the same engine installed in the Pz.Kpfw.IV, the Maybach HL120 TRM 12-cylinder gasoline engine. Producing 265 horsepower, the engine could propel the 24 metric ton vehicle up to 40km/hr to a range on roads of up to 120km. Its overall length was 5.8-meters, height 2.45-meters and width 2.86-meters. Up to 32 rounds could be stowed internally for the StuH43, which was directed using the Sfl.Z.F.1a sight. The secondary armament, a 7.92mm MG34, had a reserve of 600 rounds. Up to two MP40s were stowed for crew self-defense and the standard radio fit was a Fu.5 or Fu.2.

Sturmmörser 606/4 mit 38cm Raketenwerfer 61
Also designated Panzersturmmörser, a total of 18 of these formidable assault mortars were produced using converted Tiger I chassis, by the time the program

ended in December, 1944. The main weapon was derived from a naval anti-submarine device, which was mounted in a ball mount in a fixed casemate. The casemate featured a 150mm front plate and the bow was 100mm thick, making the vehicle all but immune in its frontal arc to conventional contemporary anti-armor weapons. The small number of Sturmtiger produced were assigned to independent units called Sturmmörser-Kompanien, numbered in the 1000-series; each was to field four assault mortars divided into a pair of two-vehicle Zuge (platoons).

Sturmmörser-Kompanie 1000 was hastily-formed and deployed immediately to counter the general uprising of the Polish Armiya Krajowa (AK, or Home Army) that centered in and around Warsaw in August 1944. It fielded two assault mortars in Warsaw; when re-organized for the Ardennes offensive in December 1944, it was equipped with only three (instead of four) of them and was assigned to 15.Armee.

Sturmmörser-Kompanie 1001 was formed in September of 1944, and in December it deployed four vehicles in the Ardennes Offensive, also as part of 15.Armee. Sturmmörser-Kompanie 1002 was formed in October of 1944, also with four vehicles; by December it was fighting against the Allies in the Reichswald where it abandoned the last of its assault mortars due to a lack of fuel and a means of recovery.

This massive assault mortar weighed in at 65 metric tons (combat loaded) and was 6.28-meters long, 3.57-meters wide and 2.85-meters high. Powered by a Maybach HL230 P45 12-cylinder gasoline engine of 650 horsepower, the Sturmtiger had a top speed of 37.5Km/hr and a range on roads of 120km. It stowed 14 rounds for the 38cm StuM and 2550 rounds for the casemate ball-mounted MG34. The main weapon was aimed using the PaK Z.F. sight, while communications included and intercom and Fu.5 radio.

On the whole, some of these later assault weapons could be considered only partially successful. Certainly the Sturmgeschütz IV was every bit as successful as its sire, the Sturmgeschütz III, in the role of a tank destroyer. The makeshift s.IG.33 proved that the concept of mounting a large-caliber weapon in a tracked chassis had merit, but there were too few of them to have an effect on the mighty struggle in and around Stalingrad. The Sturmpanzer IV refined the concept further and resulted in a robust and reliable design. Yet, it too was rarely employed in its intended role. Typically, the Germans took the next step up in size and created the Sturmtiger, a system that they no longer needed and which was deployed far too late in the war and in such small numbers, that they were never of any real use.

Towards the war's end, and as usual, Germany squandered scarce design and production resources on grandiose designs, which were thought to be able to turn the tide in their favor. That they would have little or no effect on the ultimate outcome of the conflict was not understood at the time.

Acknowledgements
The author presents his sincere thanks to the following researchers, authors, artists, webmasters and modelers for their work relating to the history of this fascinating aspect of Germany's World War Two use of armored fighting vehicles.

T. Anderson, F. Aufsess, C. Awender, M. Bitoh, P. Chamberlain, T. Cockle, B. Culver. V. Deygas, H. Doyle, G. Edmundson, R. Eiermann, H. Engel, U. Feist, W. Fleischer, S. Hards, S. Jablonski, M. Jaugitz, T. Jentz, H. Kitamura, F. Kurowski. J. Ledwoch, A. Majewski, A. Milesi, K. Mucha, T. Namie, G. Parada, B. Perrett, W. Spielberger, W. Trojca, M. Zöllner and as always, Steve Zaloga.

Any errors of fact or interpretation are my responsibility. The reader is referred to Volume 1 in this series for a select bibliography.

Additionally, my thanks go to my partner in these two books, Laurent Lecocq for his wonderful color plates and to Freddie Leung and the team at Concord for uncovering so many new and interesting photographs.

A Note on the Photographs
The photographs that appear in these two volumes came from a variety of sources. While every attempt was made to obtain fresh new images, some compromises had to be made. Therefore, in order to make the story as comprehensive as possible, within the limits of this series' format, previously-used images have been incorporated. Some of these images have been seen in my earlier Concord books, in particular the "Panzer Vor!" series. I have chosen to carry-over the captions that accompanied some of these images as well. Where necessary, corrections to those captions have been made.

A Sturmgeschütz III Ausf.A makes its way down an inclined village street, possibly in France. This assault gun is identified as an Ausf.A by the original position of the forward-most return roller; it also mounts the early idler wheel and the original drive sprocket. Note the cube-shaped stowage lockers on the rear segment of both track-guards, another hallmark of this model.

This Sturmgeschütz III Ausf.A has survived long enough to have made its way into the Soviet Union during Operation Barbarossa. It is identified by the position of the forward-most return roller and mounts the early idler wheel and the original drive sprocket. The crew has added some non-standard stowage bins to the near-side track-guard; the positioning of the rear-most one has caused the vehicle's jack to be re-located in the position seen here. The crew has also placed a canvas tarp over the casemate roof, which due to its configuration was quite leaky.

This Sturmgeschütz III Ausf.A is seen in its natural environment, accompanying infantrymen across an open, plowed field. The configuration of the suspension system identifies the model type of this assault gun. Note the ammunition box on the back of the nearest infantryman, which indicates he is part of a machine-gun section; the motorcyclist at far left will be used to scout ahead of the assault gun or to bring news of contact with the enemy to higher command echelons.

As mentioned in Vol.1 of this series, the Waffen-SS deployed a single Batterie composed of Sturmgeschütz III Ausf.A during the opening stages of Operation Barbarossa. We again see assault guns from 4.(Sturmgeschütz) Kompanie bei V.(schweren) Bataillon Leibstandarte Adolf Hitler as it moves through an urban area in Eastern Poland or the western Soviet Union, early in Operation Barbarossa. The unit insignia and Tac numbers are visible under the dust on the rear plates of these assault guns. One photo shows a side view of the StuG.III Ausf.A, which is identified by the spacing of the forward-most return roller and the cube-shaped storage box on the track-guards. Note also that the accompanying infantrymen wear Waffen-SS camouflage smocks on their bodies and camouflage covers on their steel helmets.

Although it would appear that this photograph depicts a Sturmgeschütz III Ausf.A, it may not be the case. The stowage cube seen on the track-guard of this assault gun was fitted to early StuG.III Ausf.Bs. It would appear that the tracks are the wider 40cm types, which may mean this is indeed an Ausf.B. Note the armored cover over the Nebelkerzenabwurfvorrichtung (rack to deploy smoke candles) on the rear plate, the convoy distance-keeping tail-lamp behind the stowage cube and the Nazi aerial recognition flag covering the engine deck stowage. The horse-drawn column at left appears to consist of artillery ammunition caissons, although there are no guns in sight.

German infantrymen, many on bicycles, are accompanied by a pair of Sturmgeschütz III Ausf.Bs as they head into the heart of Stalin's Soviet Union. Although still equipped with the original idler wheel and drive sprocket, this assault gun has had the forward-most return roller relocated closer to the drive sprocket; it also wears 40cm tracks. Note the spare track sections on the glacis plate as well as the Notek black-out driving head-lamp mounted on the port-side track-guard.

This Sturmgeschütz III Ausf.B attempts to use a local tree to partially disguise itself during the advance into the Soviet Union. The Catholic style of the crosses in the cemetery indicate the Germans may yet still be in what was Eastern Poland until Stalin's Red Army "liberated" it in 1939. The Ausf.B is identified as such by the spacing of the forward-most return roller; the dust obscures the drive sprocket type.

The near Sturmgeschütz III Ausf.B has the Maltese Cross insignia of Sturmgeschütz-Batterie 660 on the port-side mud-flap. Note the tow cables on the engine deck as well as the Nazi aerial recognition flag; the Nebelkerzenabwurfvorrichtung (rack to deploy smoke candles) on the rear plate has been provided with an armored guard.

This rather undistinguished Sturmgeschütz III Ausf.B sits parked in the shade of some trees, somewhere on the Ostfront. Like many others of this model, it has the original drive sprocket, which has had a spacer ring installed between its two halves to accommodate the 40cm-wide tracks; the front return roller has also been moved further forward. It would appear from photographic evidence that not all assault guns were fitted with the wood antennae stowage troughs; they are not fitted here. Finally, note the white-painted edge of the rear mud-flap, which was an aid for low-light driving.

Having bypassed the damaged bridge in the background, this Sturmgeschütz III Ausf.B moves along the river's bank on its way to a fording point. It wears a large white-outline Balkenkreuz national insignia on the casemate side; what appears to be a large letter "B" can be seen on the forward part of it. This was the gun-in-battery letter and was seen on the opposite side as well as on the rear plate. This apparently veteran crew wears their steel helmets against surprise actions by the enemy; they have also added extra protection to the bow of their assault gun in the form of two lengths of spare track.

This Sturmgeschütz III Ausf.B tries to "lose itself" against the background as it stands ready to move forward. It mounts the new drive sprocket, which could only be used with the 40cm-wide tracks; the earlier drive sprocket could also be used with the track, but it had to have a spacer ring installed between its inner and outer halves so its teeth could engage the openings in the track faces. Note also the re-located forward-most return roller and the original idler wheel. The latter could be used with either track type without any modifications.

A smiling crewman poses next to his Sturmgeschütz III Ausf.B, affording an excellent view of the new style of idler wheel, which was introduced during production of this model. Other details of interest are the two traffic signal wands poking out of the stowed road-wheel that's mounted on the track-guard, the wooden parapet attached to the edge of the engine deck to contain stowage items and the foul weather tarp covering the casemate roof.

Barely visible under the dust, the Bison insignia of Sturmgeschütz-Abteilung 191 can be seen on the far mud-flap of this Sturmgeschütz III Ausf.B; the insignia is also visible on the armored radio pannier on the port side of the casemate. This StuG.III Ausf.B mounts the newly-introduced drive sprocket with its associated 40cm-wide tracks. The crew has covered the casemate and the opening around the gun mantlet with the specially-fitted tarp, in this case to keep the dust out. Note also the opened access hatch lids over the transmission, which was an expedient means of providing extra cooling for it and the vehicle's interior.

Moving at high-speed, a Sturmgeschütz III Ausf.B belonging to Sturmgeschütz-Abteilung 192 passes a column of trucks, accompanied by another assault gun in the near distance. Although the unit's "Skull and Crossbones" insignia is obscured by a coat of dust, the unique style of the Tac number on the casemate, as well as the wooden beams stowed on the track-guards positively identifies the formation.

This Sturmgeschütz III Ausf.B was previously misidentified by this author as an Ausf.A. It is clearly identified as an Ausf.B by the spacing of the re-positioned forward-most return roller. The early drive sprocket, narrow 36cm track, narrow road-wheels (note the spares) were also fitted to Ausf.Bs as originally produced; the stowage cubes on the rear of the track-guards were fitted to some early Ausf.Bs as well. Note that it does not mount a Notek black-out driving head-lamp and that it is missing its middle return roller. It wears a thin, white-outline balkenkreuz national insignia, and is painted in a base coat of Dunkelgrau RAL 7021.

While civilians, seemingly unimpressed by their presence move about, a pair of what appears to be Waffen-SS infantrymen crosses an intersection in a Soviet city in the company of a Sturmgeschütz III. The assault gun is quite probably an Ausf.B, but it is impossible to determine which from this angle; note the stowage on the rear deck. The "character" of this scene, including the buildings, cobble-stone street and Tram-car tracks would form the prefect basis for a scale-modeler's diorama.

A Sturmgeschütz III Ausf.B descends from a rise down to a road as it follows a mate alongside a convoy. Note how the "landing" has been reinforced with wood planks and the variety of wheeled vehicles backed-up on the road. The Sturmgeschütz is marked with a white-outline three-digit Tac number, 122, on the casemate side supplemental armor plate, as well as a white-outline Balkenkreuz national insignia. The Tac number suggests that this gun belongs to a battalion-sized unit; there were 11 such units deployed at the beginning of Operation Barbarossa.

A column of extremely dusty Sturmgeschütz III Ausf.Bs advances across the Soviet steppes. The configuration of the casemate, particularly the front section, identifies this as a StuG.III Ausf.B. Rather unusually, the commander of this assault gun is wearing goggles to protect his eyes from the dust; this was extremely rare among German motorized troops, with the exception of motorcycle drivers and sometimes their passengers.

A crewmember of this StuG.III helps a Pionier (assault engineer) as they gingerly stow an M1941 flamethrower on the engine deck. Several details of the rear of this assault gun are visible; note the configuration of the area where a missing mud-flap would have been on the rear end of the track-guard, as well as the bolted flange that connected the engine deck/superstructure assembly to the hull. The bolts were un-fastened so that the entire assembly could be removed for an engine change. Note also parts of a vehicle name on the armored cover for the rear-mounted Nebelkerzenabwurfvorrichtung (rack to deploy smoke candles).

This Sturmgeschütz III Ausf.B is from the earlier part of the production run as evidenced by the stowage cubes on both track-guards. It has been fitted with the newer drive sprocket to accommodate 40cm-wide tracks. Note the large amount of stowage strewn about on the engine deck, to include a holding "fence" made from spare track sections and a Nazi flag to prevent aerial fratricide; two spare road-wheels are also attached to the casemate side wall. This assault gun is seen crossing a typical German engineer's bridge made from pre-fabricated components.

A Sturmgeschütz III Ausf.B takes a position in an open field after having crossed an enemy barbed-wire barrier, while artillery bursts in the background. The Ausf.B featured a "tunnel" with baffles on the gunner's side which led to his Sfl.Z.F.1 gun sight, as seen here on the port side of this Sturmgeschütz; this configuration was a hold-over from the Ausf.A, but was eliminated in the follow-on Ausf.C/D.

The autumn of 1941 on the Ostfront brought on the "Rasputitsa", the thick clinging mud created by heavy rains. This Sturmgeschütz III Ausf.B belonging to Sturmgeschütz-Abteilung 192 stands by, while a Gruppe (section) of infantrymen performs for the Propaganda-Kompanie (PK) photographer. The unit's "Skull and Crossbones" insignia is plainly visible on the casemate front plate, below the Tac number. The wooden beams stowed on the track-guards were also a trademark of the assault guns assigned to this formation.

Here we see yet another Sturmgeschütz III Ausf.B belonging to Sturmgeschütz-Abteilung 192; this time it is seen earlier in the campaign moving across the steppes, accompanied by an infantryman wielding an MG34. Clearly recognizable on the near part of the glacis plate is the tactical sign for a tracked self-propelled gun, while the unit's insignia and Tac numbers are also visible in the usual places. And of course, the obligatory wooden un-ditching beams are stowed on the track-guard, along with some other items. Another fitting to note is the brush-guard located on the near-side track-guard.

As smoke rises a bit further down the road, a pair of infantrymen and a Sturmgeschütz III (possibly an Ausf.B) rest in the shadows of the trees that line the road. The assault gun is piled high with stowage on the engine deck, some of which is held in place by a parapet created by lengths of spare track. A number of details can be seen on the rear plate of the hull. These include one of the tow cable holders with its "L"-shaped retaining pin; next to that is the threaded shaft with hex-head that was used to adjust the tension of the tracks. The final item of note is the armored cover over the Nebelkerzenabwurfvorrichtung (rack to deploy smoke candles).

While he balances himself on the edge of a leichte Zugkraftwagon 1-ton Sd.Kfz.10, an assault gun crewman hands a StuK round to his comrade in the loader's hatch. This is a Sturmgeschütz III Ausf.B as denoted by the chassis number 90108 stenciled on the jack located on the track-guard. Items such as the vehicle jack were often painted with the chassis number to prevent

13

A pair of Pz.Kpfw.IIIs, apparently Ausf.Js as denoted by the shape of the rear plate, move through a small settlement on the Ostfront as a Sturmgeschütz III Ausf.B takes cover against the side of a building. This assault gun has the later drive sprocket that was introduced with 40cm track, as well as the re-located forward return roller.

A wounded soldier, accompanied by a comrade, holds on to the gun tube of this Sturmgeschütz III Ausf.B as it serves in the role of an expedient ambulance. Note that the thin spaced armor normally fitted on the port side of the casemate is missing and that a length of spare track has been fitted in its place. The Notek black-out driving head-lamp is facing towards the side and is protected by a tubular brush guard. This Ausf.B is identified by the "tunnel" arrangement for the gunner's Sfl.Z.F.1 sight; note the integral ribs that were designed to deflect bullets and shrapnel. The commander's Scherenfernrohr (scissors periscope) has been fitted with long tubes to protect the optics from the glare of the sun.

A pair of Sturmgeschütz III Ausf.Bs moves cautiously through a Soviet city as an accompanying infantryman keeps out of the line of fire. Both assault guns have the later drive sprockets and idler wheels fitted as part of their suspension systems. Each commander has also deployed his Scherenfernrohr (scissors periscope); the pair at far right has tubular sun shades fitted over the optics. The vehicle immediately to the left, in the foreground, is a leichter Gepanzerte Beobachtungskraftwagen Sd.Kfz.253 (armored command vehicle).

14

Piled high with infantrymen, this pair of Sturmgeschütz III Ausf.Bs moves towards the sound of the guns. The near assault gun features a cube-shaped stowage box on the track-guard as well as the earlier style of drive sprocket and idler wheel. It is also fitted with a convoy distance-keeping tail-lamp, seen in the cut-out within the folded-up mud-flap. Both assault guns have un-armored Nebelkerzenabwurfvorrichtung (rack to deploy smoke candles) on their rear plates.

This Sturmgeschütz III Ausf.B shows the later style of drive sprocket and return roller arrangement, as well as the typical use of a tarp over the casemate roof to keep nature's elements at bay. Note also the small white square on the wall of the armored radio sponson. The as yet unidentified unit that used this symbol also probably used a white triangle and a white ring as a Batterie identification device within the Abteilung; the latter two symbols have been seen often in photographs.

This Sturmgeschütz III Ausf.B is marked in similar fashion to the one in the previous photograph, but instead has a white ring painted on the casemate's supplementary side armor, as well as on the near-side mud-flap. A large white gun-in-battery letter, "E", is seen on the rear superstructure plate. A similar device would also appear on the forward sides of the casemate. Note the infantrymen clinging to the engine deck in order to cross the river with dry feet and the fascines laid out on the near bank to provide for a longer-lasting approach to the ford.

One crewman goes through some contortions as he shares a story with his comrades, while all gather behind a Sturmgeschütz III Ausf.B. The assault gun features the earlier idler wheel and also has a triangular Tac sign in white paint on the casemate's supplementary side armor; there also appears to be a similar marking in the crushed mud-flap behind the man, second from left. All of these men wear the Feldgrau assault gun crew uniform, of a similar cut to that worn by the Panzertruppen.

A column consisting of a pair of Sturmgeschütz III Ausf.Bs shares a road with a column of trucks, including an Opel 3-ton truck. At this distance little in the way of details can be seen on the nearest dust-covered assault gun, other than the configuration of the casemate, which identifies the model type.

Three of the four men that comprised the crew of this Sturmgeschütz III Ausf.B ride outside the vehicle as their driver speeds them along to their next destination. This dust-covered assault gun plainly shows a white "F" as its gun in battery lettor, painted on the casemate's front plate. What is likely a unit insignia is faintly noticeable on the starboard side mud flap. The crew wear the usual Feldgrau assault gun crew clothing, with, in this case, the rarely-seen padded beret, also in the same color as their uniforms.

This Sturmgeschütz III Ausf.B presents an interesting combination of features, to include a Notek black-out driving head-lamp on the near-side track-guard; this and the adjacent marker lamp is protected by a tubular brush guard. A horseshoe has been fixed to the casemate's side, above the view-port flap next to the driver's position, while a vehicle scoreboard and the insignia of StuG.Abt.243 is painted on the casemate's supplementary armor and the armored radio pannier, respectively.

Covered in dust as well as infantrymen, a Sturmgeschütz III Ausf.B makes speed towards its next destination. Note the rare use of goggles by several of the men, and that the nearest man, probably the assault gun's loader, cradles an MG34 with bipod in his lap. The crew has mounted lengths of spare track on the bow and glacis, while a cover protects the bore of the 7.5cm StuK40 from dust.

Seen during the onset of the first winter on the Ostfront, several German wheeled vehicles cross a makeshift wooden bridge, as the crew of a Sturmgeschütz III Ausf.B figures out how to extract their assault gun from the mud. They had best do so speedily; if the mud freezes they may have to abandon their valuable vehicle.

A leichter Gepanzerte Beobachtungskraftwagen Sd.Kfz.253 (armored command vehicle) leads a column of Sturmgeschütz III Ausf.Bs past a group of communications trucks, parked along a road in the Soviet Union. At first glance, especially since the half-track pulls a trailer, it may be thought to be its close relative, the leichter Gepanzerte Sd.Kfz.252 (armored ammunition carrier); however the shape of the superstructure side reveals it to be a '253. The assault guns are traveling in a tactically sound manner, leaving a certain distance between themselves as a precaution against enemy artillery as they cross an open area.

These two photographs depict "Seydlitz" (named for the Great War Battlecruiser and 18th-Century soldier), a Sturmgeschütz III Ausf.C or D, belonging to StuG.Abt.177, at two different locations and times, somewhere on the Ostfront. The assault guns belonging to this unit were colorfully-marked on the casemate side, usually with a vehicle name, unit insignia and a white outline Balkenkreuz national insignia. At a distance, it is impossible to know for certain if this is a StuG.III Ausf.C or D as the physical differences between the two are few and minute. This particular model can be differentiated from the previous Ausf.B by the shape of the front casemate, which on the near side is devoid of the supplementary armor; on the far side, the "tunnel" for the gunner's sight is no longer present, since his sight now only protrudes from an opening in the roof plate.

Another Sturmgeschütz III Ausf.C or D, also belonging to StuG.Abt.177 is shown here after being gutted by an explosion. "Derfflinger" (named for the Great War Battlecruiser and 17th-Century soldier) has lost parts of its suspension and the casemate's roof plate is nowhere to be seen. This assault gun is marked using the unit's practice of adding a vehicle name, the Abteilung's insignia and a Balkenkreuz to the casemate's side walls. Of note are the brush guards on both track-guards, which were used to protect the Notek black-out driving head-lamp, as well as the marker lamps.

18

It seems as though a wartime artist has created some modifications to the suspension of what is likely a Sturmgeschütz III Ausf.C or D. Although of relatively poor quality, this image shows a full set of markings on the superstructure rear plate. These include a three-digit Tac number (unfortunately obscured) and the unit insignia of StuG.Abt.244, a white shield with two black Maltese Crosses. A white Balkenkreuz and a Tac marking for a tracked self-propelled gun are painted in white and yellow, respectively, on the armored cover for the Nebelkerzenabwurfvorrichtung (rack to deploy smoke candles).

This image clearly shows the main difference between this Sturmgeschütz III Ausf.C or D and the previous Ausf.B. Note that the "tunnel" in front of the gunner's sight is no longer present, since the sight now only protrudes from an opening in the roof plate; the latter was now designated Sfl.Z.F.1a. The Ausf.C/D also introduced the new 40cm track, drive sprocket, wider tires on the road-wheels and idler wheels as standard production items (these were retro-fitted to earlier Ausf.Bs).

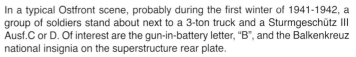

In a typical Ostfront scene, probably during the first winter of 1941-1942, a group of soldiers stand about next to a 3-ton truck and a Sturmgeschütz III Ausf.C or D. Of interest are the gun-in-battery letter, "B", and the Balkenkreuz national insignia on the superstructure rear plate.

19

A pair of Sturmgeschütz.III Ausf.C/Ds loiter in the street of a Soviet city. Note the widened new-pattern drive sprocket, introduced along with the wider 40cm tracks, seen on both vehicles. The near assault gun is heavily stowed on its engine deck, while the far one shows evidence of a scruffy winter white-wash camouflage.

A scruffy and battered Sturmgeschütz.III Ausf.C/D leads a column of wheeled AFVs including a leichte Panzerspähwagen (2cm) Sd.Kfz.222 light armored car; it appears that the remaining vehicles are a kleine Panzerfunkwagen Sd.Kfz.260 and a leichte Panzerspähwagen (MG) Sd.Kfz.221. The assault gun wears a motley coat of white-wash for camouflage, is missing a section of its track-guard and also has a gun-in-battery letter, "A", on the casemate front plate.

The commander of a Sturmgeschütz.III Ausf.C/D readies his MP40 for close-range combat as his assault gun approaches some rural structures; an infantryman stands by with his weapon "at-the-ready" to assist. Note the usual extensive stowage of spare gear on the engine deck, this time neatly enclosed in various boxes. An extra box is also fastened to the rear of the port-side track-guard, along with another on the forward end. Just behind the commander can be seen the pivot for the rod antenna, as well as its storage trough. Below his elbow can be seen the bore swab and staffs for the 7.5cm L/24 main gun. A final detail of note is the bolted flange on the superstructure rear plate. This flange, along with a similar assembly on the port and starboard sides, could be disassembled and the entire deck removed, allowing for un-restricted access to the engine compartment.

In an obvious training exercise, this Sturmgeschütz.III Ausf.C/D lets a round fly down range as a group of infantrymen huddle in a trench, parallel to the direction of fire. It is presumed that this was to acclimatize the men to the close nature of their cooperation with the assault guns. Note that the StuK is in full recoil; its report has raised a cloud of dust in front of the assault gun.

This Sturmgeschütz.III, possibly an Ausf.C or D, climbs onto a road to join a vehicle column. Typically, the crew has used spare track lengths to create a parapet on the engine deck in which they have stowed all sorts of items, including spare road-wheels. This apparently experienced crew has also attached their tow cables to the receptacles on the rear hull plate in order to shorten the time it would take to perform a recovery operation.

This detail view of the front end of a Sturmgeschütz.III Ausf.C/D shows the interesting addition of bar-stock grab handles on the transmission access hatch lids. Note also that the winter white-wash has all but disappeared, leaving vestigial streaks and blotches in many places. The road-wheel stored at right also affords a view of the mold seam normally seen on a new rubber tire, something modelers should take note of.

A Sturmgeschütz.III Ausf.C/D creates a tactically unsound cloud of dust as it moves at speed along a dry road-bed. The photographer is mounted on a vehicle that is pulling a 3.7cm PaK35/36, while the vehicle trailing the assault gun appears to be an Sd.Kfz.7 mounting a 2cm Flakvierling 38.

Preceded by a leichte Gepanzert Munitionskraftwagen Sd.Kfz.252 (light armored ammunition carrier) with Sd.Ah.51 trailer, this pair of Sturmgeschütz III Ausf.C or D crosses a shallow body of water. Note the wheeled vehicles following and the motorcyclists preparing to fan out to provide flank security.

This frontal view shows what is probably a Sturmgeschütz.III Ausf.C or D; this is indicated by the drape of the tarp over the starboard side of the casemate. Other details of note are the opened armored head-lamp cover on the port side glacis plate, as well as the ready-for-use tow cable, horn and marker lamp seen on the starboard side track-guard.

A pair of Sturmgeschütz III Ausf.Es pass a section of radio-equipped troops, somewhere on the Ostfront. The near assault gun is identified as an Ausf.E due to the addition of an armored radio pannier on the starboard side of the casemate; all previous models only had this feature on the port side. As the periods of combat lengthened, the supply situation for Germany steadily worsened. Thus, many combat vehicles began carrying large amounts of spares and consumables. The near assault gun typifies this trend by mounting spare tracks on its engine deck, which also act as a framework to keep other loose items in place, such as the buckets towards the left.

This Sturmgeschütz III Ausf.E shows some interesting additions in the way of stowage and spare tracks. The crew has placed lengths of track on the sides of the hull, most likely to mitigate against penetration of the thin armor by Soviet infantry ant-tank rifles. There is also a typical wooden box on the engine deck to hold and protect loose items. The assault gun has been given a coat of white-wash to blend into the snow-bound winter terrain; a section has been left un-painted around the Balkenkreuz and what is probably a vehicle name, which is unrecognizable due to the quality of the original image.

A Sturmgeschütz III Ausf.F belonging to the Großdeutschland division (note the "Stalhelm" insignia forward of the Balkenkreuz on the armored radio pannier) faces a Marder II Ausf.D mounting an ex-Soviet 7.62mm PaK36(r). The Ausf.F first introduced the long 7.5cm StuK40 L/43 and its large, slab-sided welded mantle, which allowed the assault gun to take on nearly every contemporary Soviet AFV it was likely to encounter. The other main fitting distinguishing the Ausf.F from any previous Sturmgeschütz IIIs, was the raised casemate roof section and the large exhaust fan cover, as seen here.

Somewhere amidst the devastation that characterized the ferocious combat that took place on the Ostfront, the crew of a Sturmgeschütz III Ausf.F stands-to for what is probably an awards ceremony. Note that the assault gun is finished in a light, two-tone camouflage finish, which is probably composed of colors seen in the second type of Tropen (tropical) scheme. The gun tube is in a darker color, which was of a special grey heat-resistant formula; normally it would be over-painted in the vehicle's base colors. The war-time censor has also painted-out the muzzle brake on the StuK40, which appears to be a rather common deceptive practice when these guns were first introduced.

This Sturmgeschütz III Ausf.F shows some features that typify the type. For instance, note the welded 30mm Zusatzpanzerung (appliqué armor) plates on the glacis and around the driver's visor. The Notek black-out driving head-lamp was also relocated to the glacis plate, as seen here. Finally, the usual custom-tailored tarp has been fitted around the welded gun mantle and casemate roof, to keep the elements at bay; note that a separate canvas cover has also been fitted to the muzzle brake.

As a group of infantrymen seek cover, this Sturmgeschütz III Ausf.F seeks to engage the un-seen enemy. Note that the StuK40 is fitted with the later bottle-shaped, double-baffle muzzle brake; this image also affords an excellent view of the raised casemate roof with its large fume extraction fan housing and cover. This assault gun is identified as an Ausf.F from this angle by the configuration of the superstructure's rear plate.

This Sturmgeschütz III Ausf.F shows two antennae, indicating that it is a command vehicle. It is identified as an Ausf.F due to the long StuK40 L/48 (here, apparently, without a muzzle brake, although it was most likely retouched by a censor) and earlier cast tow shackles on the bow. The later F/8 was based on the Ausf.J hull and had tow shackle attachment points drilled out of extensions to the hull side plates. The large raised dome for the crew compartment ventilator fan can also be seen on the casemate, between the two helmeted men in the center of the photograph. This is seen on both the Ausf.F and F/8.

The war-time censor has again removed the muzzle brake of the StuK40 mounted on these Sturmgeschütz III Ausf.Fs; the gun tube has also been shortened somewhat on the first assault gun. All are finished in the Tropen (tropical) camouflage scheme and each is marked with a gun-in-battery letter (A and B; the third is obscured). The cast tow shackles on the bow plates identify these vehicles as Ausf.Fs.

This Sturmgeschütz III Ausf.F sits on a railway flat-car while its crew poses for the photographer. In typical German fashion, the assault gun is chocked and blocked in place for travel; no retaining chains of cables are seen. The Tropen (tropical) camouflage scheme's pattern can be seen in the shadowed area of the hull side, beneath the track-guards. This is identified as an Ausf.F by the superstructure's rear plate, seen just behind the crewman with his elbow on the rear mud-flap.

A veteran poses next to his mount, a Sturmgeschütz III Ausf.F, somewhere on the Ostfront. Much like the man, the assault gun also has the look of a veteran since the experienced crew has fitted spare track lengths to the casemate's sides and starboard front plates, as well as the bow and glacis plates. Again, the cast tow shackles on the bow identify this as an Ausf.F

This well-camouflaged F-series Sturmgeschütz III has the earlier globular single-baffle muzzle brake mounted on its StuK40; note 11 white kill rings painted on the gun tube. There also seems to be mounting rails for Schürzen (skirts) on the side of the superstructure.

26

A seven-gun Batterie composed of Sturmgeschütz III Ausf.Fs parks in a tactically sound fashion at the edge of a road, using the trees for cover against enemy air and ground observers; a supply truck stands across the road from them. Note the tantalizingly undecipherable unit insignia on the glacis plate of the nearest assault gun and the man standing at far left with a traffic control wand.

This interesting and often-seen photo depicts a Sturmgeschütz III Ausf.F, which has been identified as belonging to StuG.Abt.201 on the Ostfront in 1942. It has a red Tac number, "204", painted on the pannier sides, aft of the Balkenkreuz national insignia. It is finished in the second Tropen (tropical) camouflage scheme, which was factory-applied to AFVs destined for the southern front of the Soviet Union. The StuK40 is finished in the heat-resistant grey under-coating and has white kill rings covering half its length. Again, the cast tow shackles identify this assault gun as an Ausf.F.

In this winter scene an officer, who resembles Heinz Guderian, speaks with some crewmembers of a Sturmgeschütz III Ausf.F, somewhere on the Ostfront. Although the cast tow shackle is hidden by the man behind the StuK40's gun tube, the lack of a drilled-out and extended hull side plate means that this is not an Ausf.F/8; the large fan cover on the roof also identifies this as an F-series vehicle.

This detail view of the casemate roof of a Sturmgeschütz III Ausf.F or Ausf.F/8 shows some interesting items. Note the raised roof section with the exhaust fan cover and the lack of a sliding plate over the Sfl.Z.F.1a gunner's sight opening. It would also appear that the welds on the slab-sided gun mantle are lighter than the surrounding painted metal and that the StuK40 gun tube is only finished in the heat-resistant gray paint.

A group of Luftwaffe officers, probably from the Hermann Göring division, hold a council in front of a Sturmgeschütz III Ausf.F or F/8. While almost completely obscured, this assault gun is identified as an F-series by the prominent exhaust fan cover on the casemate roof. Note also the welded 30mm Zusatzpanzerung (appliqué armor) plates on the glacis plate, along with the Notek black-out driving head-lamp.

Again, the nature of this photograph precludes precise identification of this F-series Sturmgeschütz III; the only clear feature is the raised casemate roof section with its exhaust fan tower.

The crew of this white-washed Sturmgeschütz III Ausf.F re-supplies their StuK40 with fresh rounds served up from a leichte Gepanzert Munitionskraftwagen Sd.Kfz.252 (light armored ammunition carrier). The assault gun is identified as an Ausf.F by the cast tow shackles, while the '252 is identified by the two opened hatch lids (which are still in their original Dunkelgrau base color) on the superstructure roof plate.

This Sturmgeschütz III Ausf.F/8 serves as a backdrop for a photo of these three crewmen. Note the wire anti-grenade cage over the gunner's Sfl.Z.F.1a sight opening and the Tropen (tropical) cast cover visible over the engine deck hatch lid. Of interest also is the fixed mount and insulated rubber base for the two-meter rod antenna; this was introduced with the Ausf.F/8 in place of the previous style of rotating bases.

While a rural structure burns furiously in the background, this Sturmgeschütz III Ausf.F/8 advances with some infantry on the remainder of the hamlet. The assault gun is identified as an Ausf.F/8 by the configuration of the rear superstructure plate, which was now taken from the 8./Z.W. version of the Pz.Kpfw.III chassis. It is curious that three soldiers are seeking cover behind the assault gun while another man (and the photographer) move about out in the open.

A pair of Sturmgeschütz III Ausf.Fs with what is an Ausf.F/8 (in the center) move across an open field, apparently expecting contact with the enemy. Note the different configuration of the superstructure rear plate on the Ausf.F/8 in the center of the photograph; this is a result of this model being constructed on the 8./Z.W. version of the Pz.Kpfw.III chassis. The Ausf.F introduced first the L/43 caliber StuK40 and then the L/48 caliber weapon. This was the first fitting of the longer gun to the Sturmgeschütz series; later, some older vehicles that had originally mounted the short L/24 gun were also retrofitted at workshops with the longer guns.

The Sturmgeschütz III Ausf.F/8 was a further development of the series, based on the 8./Z.W. chassis. In this photograph of a vehicle taking on ammunition, it can easily be determined that this assault gun is an Ausf.F/8 by noting that the hull sides have been extended and have had holes drilled at the upper forward edges to accept tow hooks. This vehicle also has had 30mm Zusatzpanzerung (appliqué armor) plates welded to the glacis plate and to the bow plate. Other plates have been welded to the casemate in front of the driver and on the opposite side; note the cut-out in the driver's plate for his twin periscopes. Quite typically, this vehicle also has a canvas tarp laid over the opening around the gun mantlet; this area was open to the elements, so keeping out dust, rain and cold air was its function. Also of interest are the Mittelstollen (center grousers) on the track; note the first and third link (beginning just below the near-side track-guard), which clearly shows them in place.

Four Sturmgeschütz III Ausf.F/8s form part of a load on a train headed for the front. All are covered in tarps for protection against the weather, but the characteristic bulge where the raised casemate roof section houses the exhaust fan tower is recognizable. Also visible are the cast covers over the Tropen (tropical) engine deck access hatch lids and the typical straight rear superstructure plate; these last features identify this as an Ausf.F/8. The nearest rail car holds a Sd.Ah.116 trailer, which was an item organic to the Sturmgeschütz-Abteilung's recovery Zug (platoon); it was normally hauled by a schwere Zugkraftwagen 18-ton Sd.Kfz.9 heavy half-track.

Much like many of its contemporaries, this Sturmgeschütz III Ausf.F/8 has been fitted with Schürzen (skirts) for protection against Soviet infantry anti-tank rifles. This Ausf.F/8 (identified by the drilled-out extended hull side walls) also has bolted-on 30mm Zusatzpanzerung (appliqué armor) plates on the bow, glacis and casemate front plates.

Hidden amongst this horse-drawn convoy are three Sturmgeschütz IIIs; the model types cannot be specifically identified, but since the near assault gun has the straight rear superstructure plate, it must be at least an Ausf.F/8.

In December of 1942, the first Sturmgeschütz III Ausf.Gs were produced; several features identify the nearest as one of them. The main change was the completely redesigned casemate, which featured a new armor plate arrangement as well as a new roof plate. The commander was now provided with a cupola that featured periscopes for all-around vision; note the various positions of the rotating hatch lid. The raised roof section was dispensed with, but the exhaust fan was still located there. Bolted-on 30mm Zusatzpanzerung (appliqué armor) was fitted to the bow, glacis and casemate front plates; note the space for the driver's periscopes above his armored visor. These assault guns are white-washed for concealment, and are also fitted with Winterketten (winter tracks). They are most probably from the Waffen-SS, specifically SS-Division "Das Reich", and are probably seen in early 1943 around Kharkov.

StuG.III Ausf.B, StuG.Abt.192, Ostfront, 1941
This vehicle is finished overall in Dunkelgrau RAL 7021. It is quite extensively marked, including a Tac number, white 24, on all four sides of the superstructure. In addition, the unit's Death's Head insignia is seen in all four positions, near the Tac numbers. In this case, it is probably dark green on a black square. A white outline Balkenkreuz would also be seen forward on the superstructure side plates and on the port side of the rear plate. A tactical sign, signifying a tracked self-propelled gun, consisting of an oblong shape with three vertical bars, painted in yellow, was seen on the glacis plate as well as the superstructure rear plate.

StuG.III Ausf.B, unidentified unit, Ostfront 1941
This assault gun is painted overall Dunkelgrau RAL 7021 and has white stencil style Tac number, 122, painted on the supplementary superstructure side plates. Just forward of that is a white-outline Balkenkreuz. The latter was repeated on the port side of the rear superstructure plate.

StuG.III Ausf.B, StuG.Abt.243, Ostfront 1941

Established in May, 1941, this unit saw service from the beginning of Operation Barbarossa, with its assault guns painted overall Dunkelgrau RAL 7021. Its insignia consisted of a mounted knight, in white on a red shield, outlined in white. This was typically seen on the superstructure side plates. Photographs show various playing card symbols, such as a heart or a diamond behind the knight's head on the shield. These are thought to represent the individual Kompanien within the Abteilung. The crew has added symbols in white on the supplementary superstructure plate representing their combat "kills". Twelve of these appear to be dome shapes, possibly representing destroyed pill-boxes, while the remaining three appear to be locomotives or wheeled armored vehicles.

StuG.III Ausf.C/D, StuG.Abt.177, Ostfront 1942

Photographs show that this unit applied names to their assault guns, in this case it is "Seydlitz"; another from this same unit was named "Derfflinger". The unit crest, a black griffon on a red shield was seen centered below the name, while a white-outline Balkenkreuz was seen forward and below the name; the latter was most probably repeated on the port side of the rear superstructure plate. These vehicles were finished in the standard post-June 1940 base color of Dunkelgrau RAL 7021.

StuG.III Ausf.F, StuG.Abt.210, Ostfront 1942

From March 1942, when the production of the StuG.III Ausf.F began, German AFVs pre-destined for the southern front of the USSR were often painted in the two-tone "Tropen" scheme, which at this time officially consisted of Braun RAL 8020 as the base with patches of Grau RAL 7027 covering the remaining 1/3 of the surface. This assault gun has large gun-in-battery letters, in this case "A", painted in white on the superstructure sides and front; the letter was often repeated on the rear plate as well. No other markings were seen in the photograph upon which this plate is based.

StuG.III Ausf.F, StuG.Abt.201, Ostfront 1942

This assault gun is finished in the two-tone "Tropen" scheme consisting of Braun RAL 8020 as the base with patches of Grau RAL 7027 covering the remaining 1/3 of the surface. The three-digit Tac number, 204, is painted on the radio panniers in red. Just forward of them is the Balkenkreuz in the more-or-less standard black/white style; both are likely repeated on the rear superstructure plate. The gun tube is finished in a heat-resistant grey and sports kill rings for half its length.

StuG.III Ausf.F8, StuG.Abt.243, Ostfront (possibly in the area of Stalingrad) late 1942

A number of StuG.III Ausf.F and F/8 were slated for service with Armeegruppe Süd (south) and were painted in the factory with the two-tone "Tropen" scheme of Braun RAL 8020 as the base with patches of Grau RAL 7027 covering remaining 1/3 of the surface, as seen here. The unit crest, a mounted knight in white, on a red shield is seen on the armored radio pannier, just forward of a standard black/white Balkenkreuz.

StuG.III Ausf.G December 1942 production version, 2.SS-Panzer-Division "Das Reich", winter 1943-44

The initial production version of the StuG.III Ausf.G was issued to several units, including the Das Reich division. Initially, they were painted in Dunkelgrau RAL 7021, with a winter white-wash, as seen during the battles for Kharkov in early 1943. Surviving assault guns were re-painted some time prior to the Kursk offensive in the new base color of Dunkelgelb RAL 7028. To this base color a camouflage pattern consisting of Olivegrün RAL 6003 and Rotbraun 8017 was added. A white panzer rhomboid with a vertical arrow was seen on the glacis and rear plates, on the port sides. Prior to the battle of Kursk, the temporary divisional sign of a horizontal bar with two vertical bars was applied on the bow, next to the rhomboid; this was often retained long after the summer of 1943. Vehicle names, in this case, "Florian Geyer" ("Bismarck" was another) were painted in black, above a standard black/white Balkenkreuz on the casemate side walls. The photo upon which this plate is based also shows the remains of a winter whitewash applied late in 1943.

StuG.III Ausf.G, December 1942 production version, unidentified unit, Ostfront, spring 1943

Although this version was originally issued painted in a base color of Dunkelgrau RAL 7021, surviving assault guns were repainted after February 1943. At that time, the base color of all new equipment was changed to Dunkelgelb RAL 7028. It would appear that this assault gun was repainted in the field using Olivegrün RAL 6003 as a base color, with stripes painted in Rotbraun 8017. On top of these colors, a hand-painted pattern using Dunkelgelb RAL 7028 was applied. No other markings are visible in the photograph upon which this plate is based.

StuG.III Ausf.G, unidentified unit, Ostfront, post-February 1943

The base color of this assault gun was Dunkelgelb RAL 7028. The Schürzen plates had an interesting camouflage pattern created by spraying wide bands of Rotbraun 8017, over which thin webs of Olivegrün RAL 6003 were sprayed in a zig-zag pattern. No markings are visible.

StuG.III Ausf.G, unidentified unit, time and place

This assault gun is finished in the standard post-February 1943 colors, consisting of a base of Dunkelgelb RAL 7028. To this base color was added a camouflage pattern using Olivegrün RAL 6003 and Rotbraun 8017; these are sprayed on in broad bands. A Tac number, 113 is painted in solid black characters on the Schürzen plates, just forward of the standard black/white Balkenkreuz.

StuG.III Ausf.G, unidentified unit, time and place

This extremely weathered Ausf.G appears to be painted in a monochrome scheme of Dunkelgelb RAL 7028. A Tac number, A72 is painted in red, outlined in white, on the casemate side walls, just forward of the standard black/white Balkenkreuz.

StuG.IV, unidentified unit, time and place
What appears to be a factory-fresh StuG.IV is finished on a monochrome scheme consisting only of the base color, Dunkelgelb RAL 7028. A Tac number, 123, possibly painted in red is seen on the Schürzen, aft of a standard black/white Balkenkreuz.

StuG.IV, unidentified unit, time and place
This StuG.IV is finished in the base color of Dunkelgelb RAL 7028, with broad, translucent bands of the secondary colors, Olivegrün RAL 6003 and Rotbraun 8017. The only other marking seen is a Tac number, 21, painted on the Schürzen plates. There may have been a black/white Balkenkreuz painted aft of the number, but it is obscured on the original photograph.

Sturminfanteriegeschütz 33, Panzer-Regiment 201, 23.Panzer-Division, Ostfront, spring 1943

Produced in the autumn of 1942 for use at Stalingrad and originally painted Dunkelgrau RAL 7021, surviving s.IG33s were re-painted in Dunkelgelb RAL 7028, prior to being re-issued to 23.Panzer-Division. A camouflage pattern was sprayed on using Olivegrün RAL 6003 and Rotbraun 8017; it was applied in thin translucent bands. A Tac number, in this case, G7, in black with a white outline, was applied to the center of the casemate side walls, above a black/white Balkenkreuz.

Stu.Pz.IV, Stu.Pz.Abt.216, Kursk, July 1943

The base color of this assault tank was Dunkelgelb RAL 7028, over which was sprayed a very irregular and translucent camouflage pattern using Olivegrün RAL 6003 and Rotbraun 8017 pigments. A two-digit Tac number, 55, was applied with white paint, at the uppermost rear corner of the casemate sides. This number was sometimes repeated on the casemate rear, on the starboard side armored vent cover. A somewhat elongated black/white Balkenkreuz was typically seen painted just below, and forward of, the Tac number.

About 120 of these initial versions of the Sturmgeschütz III Ausf.Gs were produced; all were issued to units on the Ostfront and all were possibly factory-finished with a white-wash over the Dunkelgrau base color. Having survived the winter of 1942-43, this assault gun has been re-painted in the new colors issued in February of 1943, with either Rotbraun RAL 8017 or Olivgrün RAL 6003 small stripes were then added using Dunkelgelb RAL 7028. This assault gun has also been retro-fitted with a folding shield for the loader's MG34. From this angle the main identifying feature of the initial version is the two openings over the driver's visor for his periscopes; these were soon deleted on the next production batch of Ausf.Gs.

This image depicts another initial version of the Sturmgeschütz III Ausf.G; note the openings for the periscopes above the driver's visor. Another feature of this model was the angle of the sponson's front plate, which was more vertical compared to all of the later Ausf.Gs. Note also the unusual kink in the near-side track-guard, the half-white StuK40 gun tube and the bolted-on 30mm Zusatzpanzerung (appliqué armor) on the bow, glacis and casemate front plates.

This initial-production Sturmgeschütz III Ausf.G is configured almost exactly as the assault gun in the previous photograph. Another small feature of this model was the appearance of a vision port flap to the driver's left; when that was dispensed with, a small MP Stopfen (pistol port) was fitted, as seen here. Note that the crew has fitted a rack for spare tracks on the casemate side wall and that the Notek black-out driving head-lamp is missing from its mount at the center of the glacis plate.

This initial-production Sturmgeschütz III Ausf.G is also a survivor, which has lasted until the winter of 1943-44. It is named "Florian Geyer" (after a 16th-Century dissident Knight), and has been photographed several times during its career, notably at Kursk. It belongs to the Waffen-SS, specifically 2.SS-Panzer-Division "Das Reich". Note the position of the exhaust fan cover plate on the casemate roof, which from this angle is a sure identifying feature.

This initial-production Sturmgeschütz III Ausf.G advances past a burning rural structure somewhere on the snow-bound Ostfront. Its winter white-wash is rather worn, and there is typical stowage in the form of a length of track and a spare road-wheel on the near-side of this assault gun. Of peculiar note is a pintle and yoke on the casemate roof for the mounting of a machine-gun; this is a non-standard feature. Note the angle of the forward armor plates on the casemate's pannier side; this and the just-visible exhaust fan on the casemate roof identify this type.

A small series of Sturmgeschütz III Ausf.Gs were constructed on the chassis of the Pz.Kpfw.III Ausf.M, as seen here. The identifying feature in this view is the rather mangled deep-wading exhaust pipe and muffler on the port side of the rear superstructure plate. This Sturmgeschütz is covered in foliage for concealment from enemy observation and also carries a field-fabricated stowage locker on its engine deck. This Ausf.G is supported on its flank by a Pz.Kpfw.IV Ausf.G; note the style of drive sprocket on it as well as the intricate nature of its camouflage pattern.

These two photos depict a Sturmgeschütz III Ausf.G with a very interesting style of camouflage paint. It is reminiscent of the so-called "Flocage" pattern seen on some French Char B tanks in the 1940 campaign. This Zimmerit-covered Ausf.G has a factory-installed stowage rack on the rear deck as seen on later types and is also fitted with the wide Ostketten (East tracks), which allowed for better flotation on soft ground; note that the Schürzen (skirts), which are normally angled inwards towards their bottoms, are hanging vertically in order to provide proper clearance for the tracks. The second photo, depicting the assault gun crossing a shallow water obstacle, shows a unit insignia on the rear superstructure plate; it is, unfortunately, unidentified.

A column of Sturmgeschütz III Ausf.Gs approach a pair of Pz.Kpfw.VI Tiger Ausf.Es; it is possible that the assault guns are performing a retrograde maneuver (a retreat) and that the Tigers are covering their withdrawal. The main tactical draw-back of casemate-mounted guns with a limited traverse is amply illustrated here; the assault guns cannot cover their own rears. These Ausf.Gs have bolted-on 30mm Zusatzpanzerung (appliqué armor) plates on the hull, glacis and casemate front as well as full sets of Schürzen (skirts) hung on their flanks. The Tigers are marked as vehicles from 1.Kompanie of a schwere Panzer-Abteilung; note the Panzer rhomboid on the Feiffel air filter pre-cleaner on the heavy tank at right.

A later production version Sturmgeschütz III Ausf.G passes a pair of soldiers, one armed with an 8.8cm Panzerschreck anti-tank rocket launcher. The assault gun has the name "Sperber" on the cast Topfblende (pot mantle) and is coated in Zimmeret whose pattern indicates that it is an Alkett-produced vehicle. Note the addition of two cast engine deck hatch lid cowls on the glacis as extra protection. The Schürzen (skirts) on this Ausf.G have also had their edges rounded-off and are attached directly to the track-guards.

In what is very likely a "true" combat photograph, a group of soldiers take cover amongst some ruins while a Sturmgeschütz III Ausf.G spearheads the assault. The Ausf.G is identified by the commander's cupola; it also sports a extended hinged shield for the loader's MG. Quite often, as seen here, a layer of spare tracks were fixed on the rear of the engine deck to create a parapet which would hold stowage items in place; in this case it is a large wooden locker. Note also the double-stacked road-wheels on the track-guard.

A later model Sturmgeschütz III Ausf.G speeds past the ruins of some sort of industrial structure. Note the 80mm upper and lower glacis plate armor. There is a folding shield for the loader's MG34/42 as well as concrete reinforcement of the superstructure front. Note the Schürzen (skirts), with a Balkenkreuz on the forward-most panel. The camouflage very likely conslsts of a base of Dunkelgelb with large areas covered in the supplementary colors of Olivgrün and Rotbraun. The combination of Zimmerit in a cross-hatch pattern and the welded gun mantlet indicate this is a MIAG-produced assault gun.

It is readily apparent that a battle took place in this area as can be determined by the abandoned/destroyed AFVs and the derelict Soviet Maxim heavy machine gun. The Tiger II, Tac number 311, is marked as belonging to H.s.Pz.Abt.501. The Sturmgeschütz III Ausf.G in the distance has a length of spare tracks hung on the casemate flanks for added protection; from this distance no other significant details can be observed.

While a crewmember waves for the photographer, this Sturmgeschütz III Ausf.G advances across the frame. The 7.5cm StuK40 L/48 main gun is housed in a cast Topfblende (pot mantle); there are two kill rings painted around the gun tube, near the double-baffle muzzle brake. Note the spare tracks on the bow and glacis plates as well as the abundant amount of foliage that the crew has applied to their assault gun in order to hide it from casual observation.

Two boys keep their distance from a destroyed Sturmgeschütz III Ausf.G, in what is quite probably an immediate post-war photograph. This is a later production type with factory installed engine deck stowage rack and apparently all-steel return rollers. The StuK40 is mounted within a cast Topfblende (pot mantle); note the Heckzurrung (external travel lock) on the glacis plate in the folded-down position. The assault gun has lost its roof so it is not possible to determine if it had later fittings on it.

This photograph depicts a Sturmgeschütz III Ausf.G of a later production batch with what is probably a factory-painted camouflage finish; note the relatively "tight" sprayed edges dividing the two different colors next to the Balkenkreuz on the casemate side walls. This assault gun has been fitted with a factory-installed stowage rack on the engine deck and mounts one of three styles of all-steel return rollers; note also the cast deflector welded in front of the commander's cupola.

This Sturmgeschütz III Ausf.G is either being towed, or is towing another vehicle as can be seen by the taut cable hooked onto the hull rear plate. It has the cast deflector welded in front of the commander's cupola, mounts rubber-tired return rollers and Schürzen (skirts). Note the opened filler port on the rear superstructure plate as well as the tube-shaped convoy tail-lamp on the near track-guard.

Parked in a street, this Sturmgeschütz III Ausf.G exhibits an odd Schürzen (skirts) arrangement. Note that the front and rear plates are not tapered downwards on their upper edges; they are all center plates. There is concrete armor on the near front section of the casemate as well. This assault gun is also relatively unusually-marked on the side plates to include a Balkenkreuz, Tac number (131) and unit insignia from StuG.Abt.600. This particular unit was organized in December 1941 by combining Sturmgeschütz-Batterien 660, 665 and 666. The camouflage scheme is also a bit out-of-the-ordinary as it appears to be based on an overall dark color (either Rotbraun RAL 8017 or Olivgrün RAL 6003) with a horizontal swathe of a lighter color, which should be Dunkelgelb RAL 7028.

Moving through the rubble of a city, this foliage-covered Sturmgeschütz III Ausf.G exhibits a rather clear camouflage pattern on its Schürzen (skirts) plates. The colors should be a base of Dunkelgelb RAL 7028 with large cloud-shaped areas of Rotbraun RAL 8017 and/or Olivgrün RAL 6003; there also seems to be quite a bit of wear on the plates as attested by the large areas in a lighter tone.

A small convoy of horse-drawn supply wagons passes a column of white-washed Sturmgeschütz III Ausf.Gs. The first assault gun shows the standard position of the Notek black-out driving head-lamp as well as the folding shield for the loader's MG (in this case, laid flat on the superstructure roof). The StuK40 has a cover over the muzzle brake and is locked in the travel position; later Ausf.Gs also featured an external travel lock just to the left of the Notek lamp. This assault gun also has Schürzen (skirts) hung on the sides, and carries a 200-liter fuel drum on the engine deck, among other stowage items.

Seen in a town somewhere on the Western Front, a pair of soldiers dash past a column of three Sturmgeschütz III Ausf.Gs. The near man carries a Panzerfaust hand-held disposable anti-armor weapon, while his following comrade is armed with a StG44 assault rifle. The assault guns are Alkett-produced vehicles as exhibited by the waffle-plate Zimmerit pattern and the cast Topfblende (pot mantle). The nearest Ausf.G has single 80mm-thick plates on the bow, glacis and starboard side of the casemate; the 30mm Zusatzpanzerung (appliqué armor) plate over the driver's visor was always a separate bolted item, since the visor was designed to sit within a 50mm-thick plate. Finally, note the Heckzurrung (external travel lock) on the glacis plate in the folded-down position, the cast shield welded in front of the commander's cupola and the total lack of frames to mount Schürzen (skirts) plates.

The most unique thing about this Sturmgeschütz III Ausf.G is the fitting of the triple-tube Nebelwurfgerät (smoke candle discharger) mounted on the forward edges of the casemate. These were fitted for only a short time on many different German AFVs, but were apparently removed due to complaints from users. Typical for its type it mounts bolted 30mm Zusatzpanzerung (appliqué armor) on the superstructure front, glacis plate and bow plate; Schürzen (skirt) plates are also fitted.

This Sturmgeschütz III Ausf.G lays in wait in an orchard, using the trees as cover. This assault gun has the added 30mm Zusatzpanzerung (appliqué armor) bolted-on to the superstructure front, glacis plate and lower bow plate, which, with the base armor being 50mm-thick, gave it a total of 80mm of protection in its frontal arc. The distinctive commander's cupola is visible here as is the slab-sided welded gun mantle. Note that there is a tarp covering the mantle, a common sight since the area around it (even though there were baffles to prevent shrapnel or shot "splash" from entering the fighting compartment) was open to the elements, such as heat, cold, dust, rain and snow. Note the "C"-shaped tow hook attached to the port-side tow point, which itself was produced by extending the hull side plate and drilling a hole.

Approximately one-dozen Sturmgeschütz III Ausf.Gs move along a road in the Soviet Union, while a small supply column consisting of 3-ton Opel Blitz trucks, led by an Sd.Kfz.11, moves in the opposite direction. The nearest StuG.III has a set of markings on its rear plate which seem to consist (from left to right) of an "H" (which may be the gun's place in its Batterie), a Balkenkreuz national insignia and a unit insignia. The piece hanging below the plate is the exhaust deflector. It would also appear that the loader of this Ausf.G is taking no chances and has protected his flank with an extra piece of Schürzen (skirt) plate. The second photo is quite likely depicts the same unit's assault guns; this time they have deployed for action.

All three of these Sturmgeschütz III Ausf.Gs have had their frontal arcs given the enhanced protection of a layer of concrete. In addition, the crews have used lengths of spare tracks to further thicken their armor; note that some links are from Soviet T-34 medium tanks. All have their loader's MG shields in the erected position, with MG34s deployed. As a final note, the assault gun at far left has the slab-sided welded mantlet, while the other two are fitted with the cast Topfblende (pot mantle).

It is still not widely realized that Germany's Wehrmacht (national defense forces) depended to a great degree on horses for transport; the Propaganda Ministry always portrayed these forces as a technologically advanced, mechanized entity. These two images depict the same Sturmgeschütz III Ausf.G; the first one shows a mounted courier delivering a message. He is armed with a pistol and wears a map case for carrying documents; it is possible he is from the local infantry unit that is being supported by the assault gun. The other photo shows the various later fittings seen on the Ausf.G, to include cast Topfblende (pot mantle), cast armored guard welded in front of the commander's cupola, and a layer of concrete on the front of the casemate. Other features include Schürzen (skirts) on their hanging frame and a folding shield for the loader's machine-gun. Note that the crew has also added tracks from a Soviet T-34 medium tank on the bow plate for enhanced protection.

The crew of this very well-hidden Sturmgeschütz III Ausf.G appears to be performing some maintenance on the port-side drive sprocket. This is an Alkett-produced assault gun as indicated by the combination of a waffle-plate Zimmerit pattern and cast Topfblende (pot mantle).

In order to provide more destructive power against fortifications and structures, a variation of the standard 10.5cm l.FH18 was mounted on the Sturmgeschütz III Ausf.G, resulting in the designation Sturmhaubitze 42. This assault howitzer was produced by Alkett as the waffle-plate Zimmerit pattern indicates. It mounts the StuH42 within the slab-sided welded mantlet; note the muzzle brake style, which was typically seen on the field-piece as well. This assault howitzer has also been constructed with the aperture for a Rundumfeuer (360-degree traverse MG mount) on the casemate's roof plate; this would also be accompanied by Nahverteidigungswaffe (close defense weapon), but it cannot be seen in this view. Along with those modifications, the loader's hatch lid would have been reconfigured to open to either side, rather than fore-to-aft. There is a triangle-shaped plate at the edge of the near-side track-guard, which was part of the mounting system for Schürzen (skirt) plates, and finally there are two different styles of all-steel return rollers fitted to the suspension system.

At first glance this image seems to depict a standard Sturmgeschütz III Ausf.G. However, due to the bulky nature of the cover on the main gun's muzzle brake, the photo may actually be of Sturmhaubitze 42; the author is un-decided. Of note are the markings on the superstructure rear plate. At far right is the tactical sign for a tracked, self-propelled Panzerjäger unit, enclosed within a box. In the center is the gun-in-battery letter, in this case an "L", outlined in white; the inner color is uncertain. Finally, a fairly standard white/black Balkenkreuz is seen at left; note another on the upper segment of this assault gun's Schürzen (skirts). Interestingly, a dispatch-rider's motorcycle has been stowed on the near track-guard; a camouflage pattern can be seen on the bike's wheel forks and fuel tank.

This image of this Sturmgeschütz III Ausf.G is from a familiar set of photographs showing it, and the schwere Zugkraftwagen 18-ton Sd.Kfz.9 at rear, hauling a small tug-boat onto dry land. The assault gun is a fairly standard early production type with features common in mid-1943. These include bolted-on 30mm Zusatzpanzerung (appliqué armor) on the bow, glacis and casemate front plates. Bracing for Schürzen (skirts) are fitted as is the folding MG shield. The less-commonly-seen triple-tube Nebelwurfgerät (smoke candle dischargers) are mounted on the forward edges of the casemate. The insignia identifies this Ausf.G as belonging to StuG.Abt.303.

Bulgarian infantrymen (some walking, others riding) accompany a Maybach T-III (Sturmgeschütz III Ausf.G) through hilly terrain. Note the prominent St. Andrew's Cross, a black "X", on the superstructure's rear plate; it appears to be on a white background. Note the bit of the assault gun's registration number plate peeking out next to the shoulder of the man in the right foreground. This Ausf.G is otherwise very normal in appearance, to include road-wheel stowage and the mounting of Schürzen (skirt) plates on the vehicle's flanks.

A British/Commonwealth or other Allied soldier poses for a souvenir photo atop a later production Sturmgeschütz III Ausf.G. Note the 80mm-thick bow and glacis plate, the welded single-thickness 80mm plate on the casemate front, the cast Topfblende (pot mantle) and the orientation of the loader's hatches. The latter, now opening to the sides indicate that the roof plate is fitted with openings for both the Rundumfeuer (360-degree traverse MG mount) and Nahverteidigungswaffe (close defense weapon), neither of which are seen in this view. The suspension system has been fitted with all-steel return rollers, while the drive sprocket is typically minus its hub cap.

Seen in a workshop unit's area, a Sturmgeschütz III Ausf.G sits next to a repair shed. The near vehicle appears to be a captured British type, while at far right, the gun tube and drive sprocket of a Marder III can be seen. At first seemingly rather plain with only bolted-on 30mm Zusatzpanzerung (appliqué armor) on the casemate front, bow and glacis plates and Schürzen (skirt) plates on its flanks, a closer examination will reveal the widened Ostketten (east tracks) mounted on the assault gun's suspension system.

This Sturmgeschütz III Ausf.G is based on a hull that is fitted with an 80mm bow and glacis plate. In contrast, the 30mm Zusatzpanzerung (appliqué armor) on the casemate front plates are both bolted to the base of 50mm. The crew has white-washed their assault gun for winter operations; they have also stowed track links on the hull side plates for added protection; these were only 30mm-thick and could easily be pierced by armor-piercing shot from the then-current Soviet infantry anti-tank rifles. The official response to that threat was the introduction of Schürzen (skirts); mounted on the vehicle's flanks, these were designed to mitigate the rifle's effects. Only the frames for them are fitted to this assault gun.

A pair of Soviet Red Army soldiers cautiously reconnoiter the area around what is apparently a gated military installation; note the typically red, white and black-striped booth for the guard. At far right is a Sturmgeschütz III Ausf.G, while an ex-French Renault R-35 reconfigured as a Munitionschlepper 35R (ammunition carrier) or Artillerieschlepper 35R (gun tractor) by the Germans, is parked closer to the gate.

A US Army cinematographer examines a destroyed Sturmgeschütz III Ausf.G, somewhere on the Western Front. It appears that the assault gun was struck from the opposite side; note the track behind it and the pair of spare road-wheels at far right that have had their rubber burned away. Stowage items on the engine deck include 20-liter jerry cans, while spare track lengths are seen on the casemate's rear and side plates.

This line-up of Sturmgeschütz III Ausf.Gs are later versions, although the application of Zimmerit would place them in batches produced before September, 1944. The first thing of note is that they all have non-standard supplementary armor plates fitted on top of their track-guards, covering the sides and the forward corners of their superstructures. The first assault gun features the later cast Topfblende (pot mantlet) and the later superstructure roof plate with modified loader's hatch lids, which open to the sides rather than fore-to-aft as on earlier Ausf.Gs. This vehicle should also have the mountings for a Rundumfeuer (360-degree traverse MG) and the Nahverteidigunswaffe (close defense weapon) on the new roof plate. Sturmgeschütz were often shipped to the troops without either of these devices due to production shortfalls; regardless, the mounts were there, often covered by a plate. This vehicle also has the newer 80mm-basis plates on the bow and glacis, as well as on the re-designed starboard-side superstructure front; the latter is composed of a single plate, rather than the earlier 50mm plate with a bolted-on 30mm plate. The driver's front plate was not changed to a unified 80mm plate since that would have required a re-design of his vision port. This vehicle also had the external gun tube travel lock next to the head-lamp mount, which in this case is fitted with a Bosch lamp instead of the standard Notek lamp.

This two photos appear to be of the same Bulgarian Maybach T-III (Sturmgeschütz III Ausf.G); taken together they show several interesting features. Beginning with the markings, the partly-obscured vehicle registration number (B60537) is stenciled in white characters directly on to the superstructure rear plate, and black characters on a white plate on the casemate front plate. The St. Andrew's Cross is painted on in black with no border. These photographs also afford a fine view of the exhaust system deflector plate as well as the baffles on either side of it, the cast shield welded in front of the commander's cupola, and the hinged forward part of the cupola's hatch lid, which allowed for the use of the Scherenfernrohr (scissors periscope) from under protection with the remainder of the lid closed. The rear deck is amply stowed with spare track and road-wheels, while the StuK40 is fitted with a cast Topfblende (pot mantlet).

What is probably a Sturmgeschütz III Ausf.G raises a cloud of dust as it moves to its next position. Note that the crew has mounted one of the Schürzen plates on the track-guard next to the superstructure, and that the rear deck is (as usual) cluttered with necessary gear.

An Auto-Union staff car (note the manufacturer's logo on the radiator grill) of a general officer stops along side a Sturmgeschütz III Ausf.G. The car carries the square pennant of a division's commander on one fender, as well as the triangle-shaped pennant of an Armee or Armee-Gruppe commander on the starboard side, just behind the head-lamp. There are several items of note on the Sturmgeschütz, including: the Alkett factory's "waffle-plate" Zimmerit pattern on the casemate side plates, double layers of cut-down Schürzen (skirt) plates attached directly to the track-guard, and a cast armored shield welded to the front of the commander's cupola (introduced in the fall of 1943); note also how the cupola hatch lid could be rotated.

While a group of Waffen-SS infantrymen take shelter in a slit trench, a Sturmgeschütz III Ausf.G with a rather unique camouflage scheme pauses while its commander makes an observation from his open cupola hatch. It appears that the assault gun is finished in a base color of Dunkelgelb RAL 7028 with wide bands of either Rotbraun RAL 8017 or Olivgrün RAL 6003; the base color was then treated to fine sprayed lines in whichever secondary color was not used for the bands. Note the use of tracks from a Soviet T-34 medium tank on the casemate's side walls, situated behind the Schürzen (skirts).

This Sturmgeschütz III Ausf.G has suffered a catastrophic explosion, which has gutted it. The superstructure has been torn from the hull, while the casemate roof is nowhere to be seen. Note also that the entire gun and its mount have been torn away with the superstructure. This Sturmgeschütz has been fitted with bolted-on 30mm appliqué armor on the glacis and bow plate and Zimmerit anti-magnetic mine paste, which appears to be applied in the cross-hatch pattern associated with the MIAG factory. With the vehicle in such condition it may be presumed that the track length seen fitted to the superstructure side has been welded there permanently as added protection, rather than for use as spare parts; there is also no visible strip or frame to hold it in place.

An American soldier poses atop the StuK40 gun tube on this Alkett-produced Sturmgeschütz III Ausf.G. Note the characteristic waffle-plate Zimmerit pattern, which along with the cast Topfblende (pot mantlet), identifies the manufacturer. The bow, glacis and starboard front of the casemate are all constructed from unified 80mm-thick armor plates. A covering of concrete affords extra protection to the upper part of the casemate, while part of a modified Schürzen (skirt) plate sits in front of the assault gun; note the Tac number, 321, next to the Balkenkreuz national insignia.

A group of infantrymen await an attack in their trench, while a Sturmgeschütz III Ausf.G lurks in the shadow of the tree-line in the background. The assault gun has the cast Topfblende (pot mantlet) for the StuK40, factory-installed stowage rack on the engine deck and loosely-mounted Schürzen (skirts) on its flanks. Note the small black and white Balkenkreuz national insignia on the forward-most plate.

A destroyed Sturmgeschütz III Ausf.G sits in the tall grass next to a river; note that the casemate's roof has been completely blown clear of the assault gun. The 7.5cm StuK40 is mounted inside a slab-sided welded mantle; Schürzen (skirts) and frames can be seen on the starboard side, while the remains of their mounting brackets can be seen on the port side.

Probably photographed in the last months of the war, this relatively early-production Sturmgeschütz III Ausf.G plays host to a soldier as he has a souvenir photo taken by a comrade. Bolted-on Zusatzpanzerung (appliqué armor) is fitted to the bow, glacis and casemate front plates. Note the patch welded low on the bow, which indicates this assault gun was previously knocked-out and repaired; it is quite probable that the concrete protection on the casemate was added at that time. An unusual Tac number, A72, has been painted on the casemate side, forward of the Balkenkreuz national insignia.

This derelict Sturmgeschütz III Ausf.G has suffered some severe and unusual damage; note the twisted muzzle brake on the bore end of the 7.5cm StuK40. The gun itself is mounted within a cast Topfblende (pot mantlet). The torn-up suspension system features all-steel return rollers as well as a drive sprocket without the armored hub-cap.

A destroyed US-manufactured M4-series medium tank (possibly an M4A4, and therefore manned by British/Commonwealth or other Allied troops) lies next to its nemesis, a Sturmgeschütz III Ausf.G, which has also been knocked-out. The assault gun has lost the casemate roof and most of the port-side suspension system. The dark spot below the upper right-hand side bolt on the welded mantlet's front plate may be an aperture for a co-axial 7.92mm MG34, which was fitted to very late-production Ausf.Gs.

Probably the most unusual feature seen on this Sturmgeschütz III Ausf.G is the length of spare tracks on the casemate side; note how several of the links are broken. This assault gun appears to be wearing a camouflage scheme in the so-called "Ambush Pattern". Other later features include the factory-installed stowage rack on the engine deck, cast armor guard welded in front of the commander's cupola, cast Topfblende (pot mantlet) for the StuK40 and suspension system components that include all-steel return rollers and a drive sprocket without an armored hub cap.

The loader of this Sturmgeschütz III Ausf.G sits with his MG34 at the ready behind its shield, while a pair of infantrymen occupies the engine deck; the commander is in his cupola hatch. This assault gun has been fitted with the triple-tube Nebelwurfgerät (smoke candle discharger), mounted on the forward edges of the casemate and the crew has also hung a length of spare track in that area for added protection. A spare road-wheel is mounted against the casemate side wall, between it and the Schürzen (skirt) plates.

A pair of US Army soldiers from the 3rd Armored Division (note the shoulder patch on the man at far right), have a look at a dead German assault gun crewman, who hangs over the StuK40 gun tube of this destroyed Sturmgeschütz III Ausf.G. An internal explosion has caused the casemate roof to be blown away. 7.5cm ready rounds in their open racks, in particular, had no extra protection from any enemy fire that pierced the main armor; they could easily "cook-off" and create a massive explosion.

A couple of Sturmgeschütz III Ausf.Gs move through "The Fog of War" across an open field. Each assault gun is fitted with Schürzen (skirts); the one at right has a Tac number, 113, on the second plate from the front, with a Balkenkreuz national insignia on the third one. A camouflage pattern of vertical, wavy bands in one or both secondary colors (Rotbraun RAL 8017 and/or Olivgrün RAL 6003) cover the base color of Dunkelgelb RAL 7028.

A later Sturmgeschütz III Ausf.G is guided onto a railroad flat-car by the man in the foreground, while others wait their turn to follow. Note that the guide has a sledge-hammer in his left hand which will probably be used to secure the various wooden beams and blocks that will keep the loaded assault gun from shifting on the flat-car. The nearest Ausf.G has the cross-hatch pattern Zimmerit associated with the MIAG factory, and the welded slab-sided mantlet for the StuK40. The bow and glacis plates are 80mm-thick as is the starboard side of the casemate front.

At first glance, this would appear to be a rather common later Sturmgeschütz III Ausf.G. It carries Schürzen (skirts), is covered in Zimmerit and has a field-constructed stowage locker fitted to the factory-supplied rack on the engine deck; it also has the cast shield welded in front of the commander's cupola. What makes it unique are the markings. These consist of over-sized Balkenkreuz national insignia on the casemate sides and rear superstructure plates; these are duplicated on the second Schürzen (skirt) plate, presumably on both sides. It also carries an over-sized Tac number, 127, on the casemate sides, which is yet again repeated on the third Schürzen (skirt) plate.

A Sturmhaubitze 42 leads a pair of Sturmgeschütz III Ausf.Gs through a treacherous, muddy area. Note the shorter, thicker gun tube of the StuH42, the Alkett-style "waffle plate" Zimmerit and the Schürzen (skirts) fitted to the lead vehicle. The two nearest assault guns also have a camouflage pattern over the base color of Dunkelgelb RAL 7028, which consists of either Rotbraun RAL 8017 and/or Olivgrün RAL 6003.

A Sturmgeschütz III Ausf.G supports a group of widely-dispersed infantrymen on the wintry steppes of the Soviet Union. Note the very small object to the commander's cupola front; it is his Scherenfernrohr (scissors periscope), which provided him with long-range vision from under protection. This Ausf.G is fitted with the earlier pattern Schürzen (skirts), which had upper and lower sections for the two middle plates and a different hanging arrangement; this can be discerned in this photograph due to the difference in the colors of the plates.

The crew of this Sturmgeschütz III Ausf.G prepares to move their assault gun out of cover and into action. It was common to park vehicles next to any available structure to help conceal it from the enemy and to afford the crew some shelter in close proximity to their AFV. This crew has removed some wooden saplings from the front of the Ausf.G and is now in the process of folding the tarp that protected it from the elements. It appears that this assault gun is finished in a base color of Dunkelgelb RAL 7028, which has been given a coat of winter white-wash camouflage.

Presumably photographed somewhere in the Mediterranean, probably Sicily or Italy, a column of Sturmgeschütz III Ausf.Gs takes a maintenance break during a road-march. They are possibly preparing to entrain, or have recently detrained, since the Schürzen (skirt) plates are stowed on their engine decks. Note that they are all in relatively pristine condition and that Zimmerit is not in evidence; the near assault gun has a few 20-liter jerry cans stowed on the starboard track-guard, a bit of track, and a box on the engine deck. In addition, a fine view is afforded of the empty fittings to stow spare road-wheels on the rear-most engine access hatch lids.

A Sturmgeschütz III Ausf.G travels along a winding path, followed by another similar assault gun, while the men riding outside do their best to stay warm. There are no discernable markings or any Zimmerit on the near assault gun, which is based on a hull with unified 80mm-thick armor plates on the bow and glacis; the casemate front plates both feature bolted-on 30mm-thick Zusatzpanzerung (appliqué armor) on the 50mm base. Early-style Schürzen (skirts) are fitted to the near Ausf.G; note the horizontally-split second and third plates, which identify the type.

Several Sturmgeschütz III Ausf.Gs occupy a dip in the terrain in an effort to mask their location from direct enemy observation; experienced crews would never willingly park on the crest of the near-by ridge in the background. The middle assault gun is an Ausf.G as can be seen by the commander's cupola. The fragmentary view of the Sturmgeschütz at far right shows two kill rings on the StuK40 gun tube as well as a modified (rounded) lower edge to the front Schürzen (skirt) plate; this was presumably done to lessen the likelihood of it snagging on something and then being torn from its mounting frame.

Obviously expecting a close encounter with the enemy (note the P38 pistol in the hand of the man at left), a pair of infantrymen accompany a Sturmgeschütz III Ausf.G as it closes in on a rural structure. This Ausf.G has the later style of Schürzen (skirts), which feature a single sheet of steel on the second and third stations; note also the factory-installed stowage frame on the engine deck, which has been further reinforced with wooden beams.

Almost completely covered with infantrymen, a white-washed Sturmgeschütz III Ausf.G passes burning wreckage, somewhere on the Ostfront. The Schürzen (skirts) are the early style with the two center segments divided in half horizontally; note the Tac number, 19, on the upper second plate. The StuK40 is mounted in a cast Topfblende (pot mantlet); note how the muzzle brake seems darker than the remainder of the gun tube.

Although it is mostly obscured by the tree in the foreground, what is quite likely a Sturmgeschütz III Ausf.G makes its way past a ruined rural structure. It mounts the long StuK40, while the hinged MG shield in front of the loader's hatch can be seen in the folded-down position. Note how this Ausf.G uses the undulations of the terrain as well as the fence in the near distance to provide concealment from an approaching enemy, and how the rural structure masks its vulnerable flank from direct enemy attack. Aside from infantry support in the assault, the StuG.III gained a well-deserved reputation as an extremely efficient tank destroyer; the position this one currently occupies is part of the reason why.

The leichte Gepanzerte Munitionskraftwagen Sd.Kfz.252 has survived in service long enough to be loading StuK40 rounds onto an Alkett-produced Sturmgeschütz III Ausf.G, which itself had to have been produced sometime after the beginning of September 1943; this is when Zimmerit was first introduced, while the pattern was that which was associated with that particular factory. The assault gun also has later all-steel return rollers and a factory-installed stowage rack on the engine deck. Extra protection has been added to the Ausf.G in the form of logs over the casemate sides and spare tracks to protect the vulnerable lower hull side plates. Both AFVs sport three-digit Tac numbers, 332 and 324, identifying them as belonging to the 3.Kompanie of the Sturmgeschütz-Abteilung.

While the battle for the possession of Stalingrad raged, Hitler, in his usual way, took a hand in proposing the design of an AFV. This design became the Sturminfanteriegeschütz 33, which mounted the 15cm s.IG33 heavy infantry gun on re-built StuG.III chassis. A total of 24 were built and many were lost with the capitulation of the German 6.Armee at Stalingrad. By April 1943, those which remained in service were assigned to Panzer-Regiment 201, 23.Panzer-Division, where they comprised a single Sturminfanteriegeschütz Batterie. One such vehicle, Tac number G7, is seen here during that spring as it passes a destroyed Soviet BM-13 "Katyushka" (Little Catherine), based on a US-manufactured Lend-Lease Studebaker US-6 2.5-ton truck chassis.

A seemingly brand-new Sturmgeschütz IV moves across an open field, probably on a training exercise. Although the original image is not of high quality, several features can be easily noted. These include the single horizontally-oriented cylindrical exhaust muffler, complete sets of Schürzen (skirts) and drive sprocket introduced on the Pz.Kpfw.IV Ausf.H. The crew has also positioned a stowage locker on the engine deck, just behind the casemate's rear wall; also of interest is the Balkenkreuz national insignia and a Tac number, 123, on the first and second Schürzen sections.

A dejected group of German prisoners slog through the mud while an abandoned Sturmgeschütz IV sits in the background. Typical for this type, the assault gun mounts its StuK40 inside a cast Topfblende (pot mantlet), has spare track on the bow and glacis plates and has bolted 30mm-thick Zusatzpanzerung (appliqué armor) on the starboard side of the casemate front plate. Empty mounting rails for Schürzen (skirts) remain in place, while the Bosch black-out driving head-lamp seen on the near-side track-guard has had its cover removed.

This line-up of Sturmgeschütz IVs is led by the rarely-photographed Befhelspanzer IV; note the rod antenna on the turret roof and the star antenna on the rear. The StuG.IVs all have the earlier folding MG shield and are fitted with Schürzen (skirts) and/or the mounting rails; there is a Balkenkreuz national insignia on the middle plate of the first assault gun.

To further supplement the supply of assault guns, Germany fielded a hybrid vehicle based on a Sturmgeschütz III Ausf.G gun and superstructure mounted on a Pz.Kpfw.IV Ausf.H or J chassis; this was designated Sturmgeschütz IV. Seen here is an earlier version as evidenced by the folding shield for the loader's MG34 on the superstructure roof and the earlier drum-type exhaust muffler on the hull rear. Note the four-digit Tac number, 4334, on the superstructure side, just forward of the Balkenkreuz national insignia. This assault gun is covered in Zimmerit paste and has lost its Schürzen (skirt) plates, although the rather distressed mounting rail and frames are still retained. Note the eagle insignia on the shoulder of the Waffen-SS soldier at left; notably, 17.SS-Panzergrenadier-Division "Götz von Berlichingen" was equipped with a full Abteilung of these assault guns

This knocked-out Sturmgeschütz IV has features seen on later production batches, such as: single 80mm-thick armor plate on the starboard side casemate front; mount for Rundumfeuer (360-degree traverse MG), Nahverteidigunswaffe (close defense weapon) and Pilze for the fitting of a Kran (jib-crane) on the roof plate. Note also the brackets for mounting spare track links on the starboard side of the casemate and the lack of Zimmerit in the usual places. This assault gun has been previously identified as belonging to StuG.Kp.1034 of the 34.Infanterie-Division, which served in Italy.

The crew of this Sturmgeschütz IV, together with the crew of a 3-ton supply truck, loads rounds for their 7.5cm StuK40 main gun using the tried-and-true "human chain" method. The StuG.IV has the often-seen addition of a concrete panel on the front plate of the driver's compartment, as well as Zimmerit paste. The crewmen appear to be wearing a tropical uniform and may be Luftwaffe troops.

A general officer (note the two parallel wide stripes on his breeches) addresses his troops using a Sturmgeschütz IV as a podium; note that the assault gun's commander still remains in his hatch, wearing head-phones. The most interesting feature of this vehicle is the translucent nature of the camouflage pattern on the Schürzen (skirts) and the Tac number, 21, on the third segment. The muzzle brake of the StuK40 has a dust cover fitted and the commander's cupola is protected by the cast shield welded in front of it.

Raising a tactically-unsound cloud of dust, the driver of this Sturmgeschütz IV moves at speed on a dirt road while the remainder of the crew ride outside. Interestingly, this assault gun has been fitted with wider Ostketten (east tracks), which when installed required that the Schürzen (skirt) plates be re-positioned vertically; they usually canted inwards towards the bottom when standard 40cm tracks were used. Note also how Ostketten have been used as spares on the bow plate.

A column of Sturmgeschütz IVs pass beneath an arch, probably in Italy in early 1944. They have most likely just detrained and are headed to the front, since they are in pristine condition, but do not have their Schürzen (skirts) fitted; the plates are probably laying on the engine deck for safe-keeping. These are earlier versions as can be seen by the application of Zimmerit and the configuration of the loader's folding MG shield.

A group of Sturmgeschütz IVs parade before the local population. All have the later style of mounting rails for the Schürzen (skirts), which feature triangle-shaped hangers; no plates are in evidence. Although difficult to tell at this distance, it would appear that many of these assault guns have the later style cast idler wheel with seven ribs. All have the cast Topfblende (pot mantlet) on the StuK40, cast armor shield welded in front of the commander's cupola, and folding shield for the loader's MG. Note that because the casemate, adapted from the StuG.III Ausf.G sat higher on the hull (to allow for clearance over the fuel tanks in the fighting compartment for the gun mount), the tray for carrying two spare road-wheels is mounted on brackets above the track-guards.

Popularly known as the Sturmpanzer, or more formally as "Sturmgeschütz IV für 15cm Sturmhaubitze 43 (Sd.Kfz.166)", this assault howitzer belonging to Sturmpanzer-Abteilung 216 is seen on display after its capture by the Soviet Red Army at Kursk in 1943. This I.Serie vehicle is built on a Pz.Kpfw.IV Ausf.E hull that has been fitted with Zusatzpanzerung (appliqué armor) on the hull sides and bow. It has been given a suspension upgrade to accept wider 40cm tracks; note the drive sprocket and idler wheels introduced on the Pz,Kpfw.IV Ausf.F, along with widened road-wheels. The 15cm StuH43 has the shorter collar around the gun tube, which was also a hallmark of this series.

This Sturmpanzer IV of the II.Serie also belongs to Sturmpanzer-Abteilung 216, which has now been deployed to Italy to counter Allied landings at Anzio. It retains bolted Zusatzpanzerung (appliqué armor) on the bow, but has been re-manufactured with the reinforced final drive and drive sprockets common the Pz.Kpfw.IV Ausf.H; note also that the collar around the 15cm StuH43 has been lengthened. The first two series' were fitted with the armored visor originally designed for the Tiger I, as seen here.

This series of photos depicts the same abandoned III.Serie Sturmpanzer IV, based on the Pz.Kpfw.IV Ausf.H chassis. It is covered with Zimmerit anti-magnetic mine paste, mounts almost a full set of Schürzen (skirts) and has a net strung across its front to break up its outline. Other details of interest are the open MP-Stopfen (pistol port with armored plug) with the plug hanging on its retaining chain, Ausf.H-style drive sprocket and final drive housing, all-steel return rollers and final style hub caps on the road wheels (to compare differences, note that the third road-wheel mounts the earlier type of hub cap). The mantle for the new Škoda-designed 15cm StuH43 is covered with a canvas cloth to keep dirt and debris from fouling the weapon's Kugelblende (ball mount); note also the newly-introduced plate that covered the opening for the fighting compartment exhaust fan, just above the gun mount. Finally, the armor arrangement and viewing device for the driver was changed to delete the Tiger I-style visor in favor of a top-mounted rotating periscope. In the first photo, US troops pass the assault howitzer in a quietly-abandoned Italian town; the second photo shows a curious local man, while the final one shows the town's inhabitants crowding around the vehicle along with US infantrymen and Military Policemen.

The ultimate wartime expression of Germany's quest for an urban combat vehicle was the massive Sturmmörser, based on the mighty Tiger I. This vehicle mounted an assault mortar, the 38cm StuM RW61, which fired a rocket-assisted projectile out to 1,600-meters. This particular vehicle is an earlier variation as can be seen by the additional bolted Zustazpanzerung (appliqué armor) on the bow. Note the counterweight fitted to the end of the projector tube; this was one of several variations.

This photograph depicts a Tiger-Mörser from Sturmmörser-Kompanie 1000 after it was knocked out from the rear by US forces in 1945. This vehicle does not have a counterweight on its projector tube, has been given a coat of Zimmerit on the bow, stern and superstructure sides (but not on the casemate itself), and also exhibits the external ammunition loading crane, which was mounted on brackets fixed to the casemate's rear wall. When not in use, the latter could be stored on brackets fitted to the engine deck; a device based on it was mounted on transverse rails on the inner face of the casemate roof to assist in moving the massive projectiles from their racks to the main weapon's loading tray.